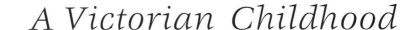

A Victorian Childhood

At Home

Ruth Thomson

FRANKLIN WATTS
LONDON • SYDNEY

First published in 2007 by Franklin Watts
338 Euston Road, London NW1 3BH

Franklin Watts Australia
Level 17/207 Kent Street
Sydney NSW 2000

Designer: Mei Lim
Editor: Susie Brooks

The author would like to thank John and Sandy Howarth
of Swiss Cottage Antiques, Leeds and Islington Education
Library Service (www.objectlessons.org) for the loan of
items from their collection, and Bella Bennett.

Photographic acknowledgements
Neil Thomson 2/3, 4t, 4c, 6t, 7, 8, 9, 10t, 12bl, 13tl, 13tr,
14, 15, 16, 18, 20, 21, 22t, 23br, 24, 25, 26, 27, 28, 31;
Martin Chillmaid/Franklin Watts Picture Library title page,
11bl, 11tc, 11br, 12t, 12c, 12br, 22br, 23cr; Mary Evans
Picture Library 10b, 17; London Metropolitan Archives 5b;
NTPL/Robert Morris 5t.

A CIP catalogue record for this book is available
from the British Library.

Dewey Classification: 640.941

ISBN 978 0 7496 7051 1

Printed and bound in Malaysia

Franklin Watts is a division of Hachette Children's Books.

Contents

THE MOVE TO TOWNS

During Queen Victoria's reign, the population of Britain almost doubled. In early Victorian times, nearly three-quarters of people lived in villages. By 1901, three-quarters of people lived in towns and cities.

Homes for workers

Life in the country was hard for poor people. Thousands of farm workers moved to **industrial** cities, such as Leeds, Birmingham, Liverpool, Nottingham and Manchester, seeking better-paid work in new factories. Streets of houses were built for workers to rent, often in the town centre near the factories and workshops.

Many houses were built joined together in rows, known as terraces. Two families lived in each of these houses – one upstairs and the other downstairs.

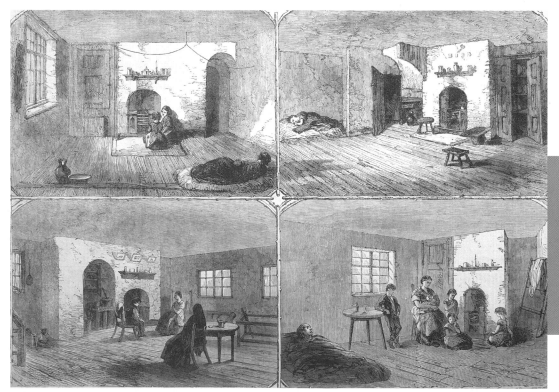

Poor families could not afford much furniture. Often, two or three children shared a bed.

Privies had a bucket, which **night-soil** men came to empty once a week.

Back-to-back houses

Builders crammed in as many homes as they could into city centres. They built houses back-to-back or in a **court**. Courts were reached from the street through a narrow passageway. These houses had no running water. Families fetched buckets of water from a standpipe or a nearby pump and shared an outside lavatory, known as a privy. Some courts also shared a wash-house for laundry.

Notice how narrow the space is between the two rows of houses in this court.

HOMES FOR POOR PEOPLE

The very poor lived in overcrowded, badly-built **slums**, which had little **ventilation**, no proper drainage, and were often filthy. Many people died young in these unhealthy conditions.

Slum dwellings

Most poor families had to share one or two rooms in cramped, often damp and draughty houses. Some even lived in dark cellars.

The workhouse

The poorest families, who could not afford rent, went to the **workhouse**. Workhouses gave people food, work and a place to sleep, but families were separated and kept apart.

Some families slept, ate and worked in the same room.

Many Victorian housing estates in London were built with funds from George Peabody, a rich American businessman.

An extract about Peabody Buildings from *The Life of George Peabody*

There were neatly tiled floors and whitewashed walls. The rooms were small, but planned economically... I noticed, especially, that each room was well lighted and ventilated. Some families had three rooms... Each floor is divided into lettered sections with spacious corridors. There are iron traps in the halls in each storey into which dirt and rubbish from each tenement [*flat*] is swept.

What does the writer like about Peabody Buildings?

Better housing

After 1875, many slums were pulled down. In big cities, new blocks of flats were built, often paid for by wealthy businessmen. These were rented out cheaply to tailors, porters, police constables, needlewomen, printers and other skilled workers.

Wealthy people and companies built almshouses – homes for poor, old people.

SUBURBS

City centres were noisy, smelly and dirty. The air was thick with smoke from factories and coal fires and there was little or no clean water. Those who could afford it moved out to **suburbs** on the edge of cities.

▲ Victorian suburban railway station

Train services

Railway companies ran cheap, early morning trains for workers. Suburban stations were built for people to travel to work into city centres. Builders put up streets of cheap homes nearby for workers to live in.

Most Victorian terraced houses were built of brick. They were cheap to build because their side walls were shared.

Terraced homes

Workers' houses were built in long terraces. Each one had a **parlour** at the front, used only on Sundays and for guests. At the back were a kitchen, a **scullery** and a **water-close**t.

Upstairs were two or three bedrooms, but no bathroom. The houses all had back yards and some had tiny front gardens, as well.

Wealthier people lived in big detached houses, called villas, with large rooms, gardens and privacy from the street.

Look out for these common features of many Victorian houses.

▲ Pillared doorways

▲ Plaques showing the name of a house or the date it was built

▲ Decorated wooden **bargeboards** with a **finial** on the top

▲ Bay windows to let more light into a house

▲ Lots of chimney pots

▲ Iron railings outside the front garden

▲ Boot scraper for wiping off mud from the streets

▲ Coal hole covers on the pavement for houses with coal cellars

▲ Sash windows that go up and down. They usually have only two or four glass panes.

COMFORTABLE HOMES

Victorian villas and town houses of the wealthy usually had three floors. Often there were attic rooms and a basement, as well. Families filled their rooms with dark furniture and lots of ornaments, and lined the walls with pictures.

Downstairs

The kitchen was tucked away in the basement or at the back of the house. On the ground floor were the parlour, the dining room and a study or library.

Upstairs

On the first floor were the main bedrooms and a drawing room where guests were entertained. On the top floor were the servants' bedrooms and a nursery for the children.

Houses were cold and draughty compared with modern ones. Rooms had thick, heavy curtains and open fireplaces.

Servants

Big homes like these employed servants. Some families had one maid of all work. Wealthy families had all sorts of servants – a housekeeper, a cook, kitchenmaids, housemaids and laundry maids.

A hard day's work

Maids had to keep a house spotless. They dusted and swept every room each morning. They filled jugs with hot water for washing. They cleaned and lit the kitchen **range**, polished boots, scrubbed the doorsteps, washed the windows, made the beds and laid and cleared the dining table. There were no vacuum cleaners, washing machines, fridges or electric kitchen gadgets, so everything in a house was done by hand.

Feather duster ▶

Sacking duster ▶

HARD

SHINE

BLACKING

▲ Boot brushes

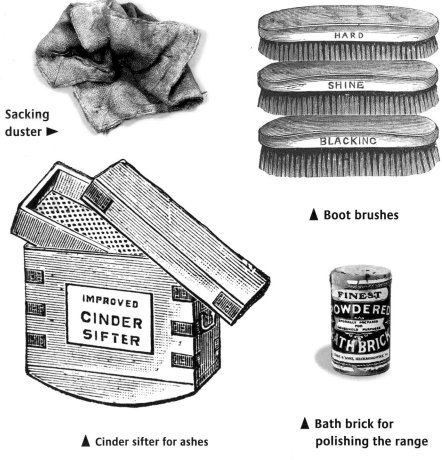

IMPROVED CINDER SIFTER

FINEST POWDERED BATH BRICK

▲ Bar of soap

▲ Cinder sifter for ashes

▲ Bath brick for polishing the range

HEAT AND LIGHT

▲ Lumps of coal

All homes, both rich and poor, were warmed with open fires. There were fireplaces in every room, which is why Victorian houses have so many chimneys.

▼ Kitchen range

An extract from *Mrs Beeton's Book of Household Management*

She [*the cook*] should first clean out of the fireplace the remains of the fire of the night before, then thoroughly brush the range. For lighting the fire she will require some paper, firewood, a few lumps of round coal, some cinders and a few matches.

The fire being lighted, the cook should clear away all the ashes and cinders, rub up with a leather the brighter parts of the range and wash the hearth; when washed quite clean, but while it is still wet, she should rub it with a piece of hearthstone to whiten it, and place the kettle on the fire to boil.

How many tasks did a cook have to do before she could boil a kettle?

The kitchen range

A large, iron, coal-fired range in the kitchen heated an oven and hobs for cooking. Water was heated in a big kettle for tea, baths and washing up. People heated heavy flat irons on the range for ironing. Coal was added all day long to keep the fire burning.

▲ Flat iron

▲ Iron kettle

Lighting

For most of Queen Victoria's reign, houses were lit by oil lamps and, later, by gas light. Oil lamps gave out a very dim glow. Gas light was much brighter. Electric light bulbs were invented in 1879, but only the very rich had electricity in their homes by the end of the 19th century.

▲ Oil lamp

The deep rim of the candlesticks caught any dripping wax.

Bedtime

People lit their bedrooms with candles. In cold weather, they put a stone hot water bottle into their bed to warm up the sheets.

▲ Stone hot water bottle

This room in a late Victorian home is lit by gas light. Notice the extra oil lamp at the back.

WASHING AND BATHS

Early Victorian houses had no bathrooms, hot running water or inside loos. By the end of the century, families who could afford it put in bathrooms, but the poorest never took a bath at all.

▲ Jug

Washing and bathing

In well-off houses, every bedroom had a washstand with a washbowl and jug. A servant brought up hot water in a can from the kitchen, and later carried the dirty water downstairs.

Chamber pots

Both adults and children kept **chamber pots** under their bed, in case these were needed at night. A servant emptied them every morning.

▲ Washbowl

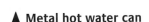

▲ Metal hot water can

People took hip baths in front of a fire, surrounded by screens to keep out draughts. The water came up only to a bather's hips.

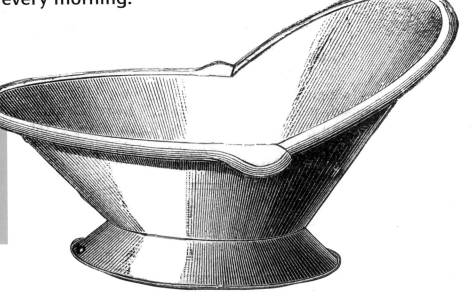

Washing for the poor

In poorer homes, people bathed once a week in a tin bath. Keeping clean was a struggle in the slums, because more than a dozen families might share a cold tap and a privy. Families rarely had a private place where they could wash and they often all used the same bath water.

▼ Tin bath

Baths and wash-houses

After 1846, some big towns built public baths and wash-houses. Here, people could have hot or cold baths in private, with clean towels and soap. There were also laundry rooms for washing clothes and linen.

Baths and wash-houses had separate baths for men and women, and a plunge (swimming) pool, used mainly by men and boys.

FAMILIES

Victorian families were much larger than today's. Queen Victoria had four sons and five daughters and the average Victorian family had six children. By the end of the century, families became much smaller.

Fathers and mothers

In well-off families, the father was the head of the family and expected his wife and children to obey him. Fathers went out to work and spent little time with their children. Mothers did not need to work. They stayed in the house, organising servants, planning meals and creating a comfortable home.

Photographs often emphasise family roles. Here, the father and eldest son stand over the rest of the family. The eldest daughter sits next to her mother.

Everyone in this poor family is helping to make matchboxes.

Working families

In poorer homes, men were paid too little to support their family, so wives and children also had to work hard. Some families worked together at home, making boxes, brushes and other small things.

Children at work

Many children worked long hours in factories, mills or in the street, until laws were passed to stop them. Even once schooling became **compulsory**, many children still worked, as well.

Extract from an interview with a headmaster in *Living London*

'He [*This boy*] was up at five o'clock this morning, and out with the milkman on his round. This evening he will be selling papers. You know, these poor children are not put to bed as early as yours are. They don't get a fair average of sleep for growing children, and when they have to work before and after school, to add a little to the family earnings, you can't expect them to have very much energy left for their work when they come to school. It is pitiful.'

Why does the headmaster feel sorry for poor children?

BABIES

Many mothers had a new baby year after year. They usually had their babies at home. There was little medical care. Many mothers died in childbirth and their babies often died, too.

Little mothers

In poor families, the older girls helped look after the babies and younger children. Many girls were kept back from school to help at home – especially on washday or when their mother went out to work.

These girls are helping their mother dress their younger sisters for going out.

An extract from
The Mother's Thorough Resource Book

The dress of an infant should be light, loose, easy, and warm. A belly-band of flannel should be worn for the first three or four months. It is a great preservative against colds. A petticoat is next required, which should be wide enough to wrap around the feet. An outer garment and a pair of knitted socks and cotton shirts complete the indoor wardrobe. For outdoor wear, a hood, robe, cape, veil and gloves will be added.

How does this baby clothing compare with that of today?

Nannies and nurse maids

Well-off families employed a live-in nanny who took total charge of the babies and young children. Some had a nurse maid as well. Nannies bathed, dressed, fed and looked after the children in the nursery. In big houses, there were two nurseries – one for daytime play and meals and one for bathing and sleeping at night.

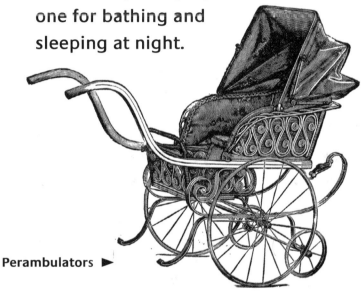

◄ **Perambulators** ►

Victorians thought that fresh air was healthy for babies. Nannies took them for daily rides in a **perambulator**.

HEALTH AND ILLNESS

In overcrowded towns, which had open drains and dirty water supplies, deadly diseases spread rapidly. For much of Victoria's reign, frequent **epidemics** of **cholera** and **typhoid** killed thousands of people.

Dirty water

A report in 1842 revealed that more than half the towns in Britain had dirty water. In 1853, John Snow, a doctor, proved that cholera was spread by dirty water. Gradually, people recognised that clean water was essential for people's health. After 1875, pipes were laid to bring clean water straight into homes and sewers carried away waste. Rubbish collections also began, so streets became much cleaner.

▲ The doctor's visit

▲ Advertisement for a ready-made cure

Medical treatment

Doctors charged fees, so only the wealthy could afford a doctor's visit. Most people treated illnesses with home-made remedies or medicines from a chemist. Some of the ready-made cures were useless and advertisements for them made all sorts of untrue claims.

▲ Free gift from the makers of Mrs Winslow's cough mixture

Children's health

Children, both rich and poor, often caught dangerous diseases, such as diphtheria, measles, smallpox, scarlet fever and whooping cough.

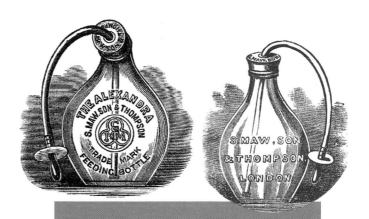

Early feeding bottles had long tubes, which were hard to clean. Germs collected in the tubes and made babies ill.

Victorians told relatives and friends of a child's death by sending them a printed memorial card.

In Loving Remembrance of

Emeline Clarice Gilbert

Died September 11, 1891. Aged 1 Year 26 Days

IN
Loving Memory of
WILLIE WHITEMAN,
THE BELOVED CHILD OF WALTER & MARY WHITEMAN,
WHO DEPARTED THIS LIFE
On the 19th, of January, 1878,
AGED 1 YEAR & 3 MONTHS.
"Jesus said, suffer little children to come unto me."

Baby deaths

More than a quarter of all babies died before their first birthday. Many died from diarrhoea, caused by dirty milk or water. Some were accidentally poisoned by a drug given to keep them quiet. Many young children also died, especially those who were weak and underfed.

Extract from
The Book of the Home

BABY AILMENTS

Bronchitis When young babies get bronchitis it is owing to carelessness in keeping them out late at night, or exposing them to fog, east wind, or draughts while washing. The complaint is extremely dangerous. If all children from birth wore woollen underclothing with high necks, long sleeves and long stockings and had double-breasted flannel nightgowns or sleeping suits, the present very high death-rate among children from chest complaints would be reduced considerably.

What does this writer consider to be the causes of bronchitis and what cure is suggested?

CLOTHES

Rich and poor children wore very different clothes. Poor children had to wear ragged cast-offs. Wealthy children had new clothes especially made for them, copying adult fashions of the time.

Clothes for the very young

Babies and small children were often dressed in white. Little boys wore dresses until the age of five or six, when they were breeched (allowed to wear trousers). Girls grew their hair long and wore it loose or tied back with a ribbon.

The young children on the left are both boys. Sometimes, mothers let their boys' hair grow long, like the girls'.

▲ Boys' fashion in the 1880s

Girls' and boys' clothes

Well-off girls wore shorter versions of their mothers' clothes. When they were about 16, they started wearing long skirts and put up their hair. Boys wore short trousers called breeches and white shirts with detachable collars, which could be removed for washing.

▲ Girls' fashion in the 1870s

▲ Detachable collar

▲ Children wearing tartan ▲ Boy in a sailor suit

Followers of fashion

The Royal family influenced children's fashion. In 1844, Queen Victoria and Prince Albert bought Balmoral Castle in Scotland and spent holidays there. The royal family often dressed in tartan and this encouraged other families to follow suit. Sailor suits became popular for boys after the Prince of Wales was painted in one.

When *Little Lord Fauntleroy* was published in 1886, it started a fashion for boys to wear velvet suits with white, lacy collars, like the character in the book.

Clothes washing

Clothes were washed by hand. This took several days. White clothes were boiled in a copper boiler over a coal fire. Other clothes were washed in a tub and scrubbed on a washboard. Wet clothes were wound through a mangle. This pressed out some of the water before the clothes were pegged out to dry.

▲ Copper boiler in a scullery

Ironing

Clothes were ironed with a flat iron. People used two irons – heating one up on the kitchen range, while they ironed with the other one.

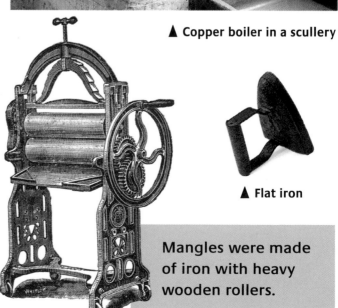

▲ Flat iron

Mangles were made of iron with heavy wooden rollers.

KEEPING IN TOUCH

At the start of Victoria's reign, the only way for people to keep in touch was by letter. The person who received a letter paid for the postage, which was costly and depended on how far a letter had travelled.

The Penny Post

In 1840, Rowland Hill invented the idea of postage stamps. The cost of sending a letter anywhere in the country was one penny.
The first stamp was known as a 'Penny Black'. Post boxes were put on the streets and letter-carriers collected, sorted and delivered letters, just as postmen do today.

The Post Office persuaded people to fit letter boxes in their doors so letters could be delivered.

Postal districts

Streets were given name plates and houses numbers, so postmen knew where to deliver letters. To make sorting easier, big cities were gradually divided into postal districts.

The first post boxes were green. In 1874, they were painted bright red. Notice the initials VR on the front. These stand for Victoria Regina (regina means queen).

Letters and greetings cards

With cheaper postage, many more people started sending letters. They also sent birthday, Christmas and fancy Valentine cards.

Postcards

In 1870, the Post Office introduced an official postcard with a stamp already printed on it. Postcards cost half the price of sending letters, so they soon became very popular. At first, postcards were plain, with room for the address on one side and a message on the back. Later, they were printed with pictures.

The first Christmas card was sent in 1843. Sending Christmas cards soon became a popular custom.

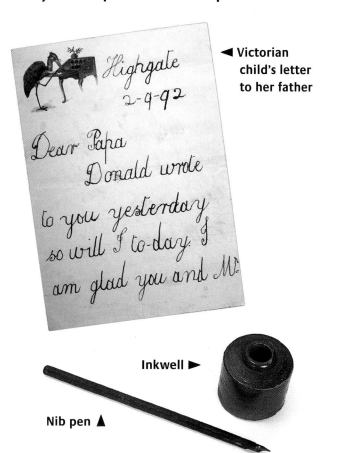

◄ Victorian child's letter to her father

Inkwell ►

Nib pen ▲

Writing

People wrote with pen and ink. Children learned to write in a style known as **copperplate**. Typewriters were invented in 1874. They were mainly used by businesses for bills, orders and letters.

Telegraph and telephone

In 1844, Samuel Morse invented a way of sending messages in a code of dots and dashes over electric telegraph wires. Operators translated the code into written messages known as telegrams. Telephones were invented in 1876, but they were not common in Victorian homes.

FINDING OUT MORE

Look around your own area for Victorian houses, post boxes, street names and other evidence of everyday life in Victorian times.

Houses

Choose a Victorian house to look at closely. Draw a picture of it and label its features.

Make a note of any modern additions, such as a TV aerial, a satellite dish or a glass porch.

Slate roof

Finial

Several chimney pots

Decorative brickwork in contrasting coloured bricks

Date or name plaque

Bay window with two or four glass paned sashes

Decorated plasterwork

Decorated pillars

Door with glass panels

Census forms

Find out from **census** forms at your local record office who once lived in a particular house in your area. Census forms list the names of everyone in a house, how they were related, their age, gender and job.

Compare households

The census is taken every ten years. You could compare the information about a house in different census years to discover whether the number of its inhabitants changed. Did people have more or fewer children later on?

Photographs

Victorian photographs will show you what people wore. Remember that most people posed in their best clothes at a photographer's studio. Later, people owned their own cameras and took outdoor pictures, like the one on the right.

Gravestones

See if you can find any Victorian children's gravestones in your local churchyard. Notice how old children were when they died. You may find that more than one child from the same family died young. How many were still babies?

Street names

Street names can give a clue as to when houses were built. Some streets were named after Victoria or Albert (Victoria's husband), or after Victorian prime ministers, such as Palmerston, Disraeli, Gladstone or Salisbury. Streets were also named after battles that the British won in the **Crimean War**, such as Alma or Inkerman, or after famous Victorians, such as David Livingstone who explored Africa, Florence Nightingale, who looked after soldiers in the Crimea, or Lord Raglan and Lord Cardigan, soldiers who fought in the Crimea.

TIMELINE

1830s

1837 Queen Victoria came to the throne.

1840s

1840 Rowland Hill invented the Penny Post.

1842 Edwin Chadwick wrote a report about sanitary conditions of working people.

1843 The first Christmas card was sent.

1848 The first Public Health Act set up local boards of health to improve sanitation in towns.

1849 Walter Hunt invented the modern safety pin.

1870s

1870 The Post Office issued plain postcards.

1874 The first typewriters were sold.

1874 Post boxes were painted red.

1875 A Public Health Act was passed, saying town councils had to start rubbish collections.

1875 The Artisans' Dwelling Act was passed. It allowed slums to be knocked down, so new homes for the poor could be built.

1890s

1890 The first electric trains ran on London's underground railway.

1891 Schooling was made free.

1891 A Factory Act raised the minumum working age to 11.

1893 The school leaving age was raised to 11.

1850s

1853 Vaccination against smallpox became compulsory for children.

1854 Oil lamps were invented.

1854–1856 Britain and France fought the Crimean War against Russia.

1860s

1861 Prince Albert died of typhoid.

1861 Mrs Beeton's *Book of Household Management* was published.

1865 An underground sewage system was laid in London.

1880s

1880 George Eastman invented the Kodak box camera.

1880 Schooling for children between the ages of 5 and 10 was made compulsory.

1881 The first electric street lighting appeared.

1882 The Married Women's Property Act enabled married women to own their own house.

1883 The first dustbins, made of galvinised iron, were introduced.

1887 Queen Victoria's Golden Jubilee (50 years on the throne) took place.

1900s

1895 The first British motor car factory opened, in Birmingham.

1897 Queen Victoria's Diamond Jubilee (60 years on the throne) took place.

1899 A survey of York by Seebohm Rowntree found that a quarter of people were living in poverty.

1901 Queen Victoria died.

GLOSSARY

bargeboard a wooden board attached to the arches of a roof or a doorway

census an official count of people living in a country

chamber pot a pottery potty

cholera a dangerous, often fatal disease caused by drinking or eating dirty water, milk or food

compulsory something that must be done

copperplate a style of writing in thin, sloping, looped letters

court a group of houses built around a small, paved yard set at right angles to the main street

Crimean War a war fought near the Black Sea by Britain, France and Turkey against Russia, from 1854 until 1856

epidemic when many people catch a disease or illness at the same time

finial a decorative point on the top of a roof gable

industrial relating to industry and factories

night-soil the contents of privies, carried away at night and sometimes used for fertiliser

parlour a smart sitting room, usually the front room

perambulator a light carriage for a child, nowadays called a pram

range a kitchen stove built into the fireplace

scullery a room next to a kitchen for washing up, laundry and cleaning

slum an area of poor, badly built housing

suburb an area of housing on the edges of towns and cities

typhoid a disease carried by dirty water

ventilation a way of letting fresh air into a room or building

water-closet a small room used as a lavatory with flushing water

workhouse a place where people could eat and sleep in return for work

PLACES TO VISIT

The following places have displays, reconstructions or exhibitions connected with Victorian homes, including nurseries, kitchens, wash-houses, furniture and household equipment.

Beamish: North of England Open Air Museum
Beamish, County Durham DH9 0RG
www.beamish.org.uk

Bethnal Green Museum of Childhood
Cambridge Heath Road, London E2 9PA
www.vam.ac.uk/moc/index.html

Birmingham Back to Backs
50–54 Inge Street, Birmingham, West Midlands B5 4TE
www.nationaltrust.org.uk

Black Country Living Museum
Tipton Road, Dudley, West Midlands DY1 4SQ
www.bclm.co.uk

Blists Hill Victorian Town
Legges Way, Madeley, Telford, Shropshire TF7 5DU
www.ironbridge.org.uk/our_attractions

Cambridge and County Folk Museum
2/3 Castle Street, Cambridge CB3 0AQ
www.folkmuseum.org.uk

Cecil Higgins Art Gallery
Castle Lane, Bedford MK40 3RP
www.cecilhigginsartgallery.org

Cogges Manor Farm Museum
Church Lane, Witney, Oxfordshire OX28 3LA
www.cogges.org

Dorking and District Museum
62 West Street, Dorking, Surrey RH4 1BS
www.dorkingmuseum.co.uk

Erddig
Wrexham LL13 0YT
www.nationaltrust.org.uk

Gunnersbury Park Museum
Gunnersbury Park, Popes Lane, London W3 8LQ
www.hounslow.info/gunnersburyparkmuseum

Hove Museum and Art Gallery
19 New Church Road, Hove, East Sussex BN3 4AB
www.hove.virtualmuseum.info

Kirkstall Abbey House Museum
Abbey Road, Kirkstall, Leeds LS5 3EH
www.leeds.gov.uk/abbeyhouse

Lanhydrock
Bodmin, Cornwall PL30 5AD
www.nationaltrust.org.uk

Linley Sambourne House
18 Stafford Terrace, London W8 7BH
www.rbkc.gov.uk/linleysambournehouse

Museum of English Rural Life
Redlands Road, Reading, Berkshire RG1 5EX
www.reading.ac.uk/Instits/im

Museum of London
London Wall, London EC2Y 5HN
www.museumoflondon.org.uk

Museum of Science and Industry in Manchester
Liverpool Road, Castlefield, Manchester M3 4FP
www.msim.org.uk

Shambles Victorian Village
Church Street, Newent, Gloucestershire GL18 1PP
www.shamblesnewent.co.uk

Shugborough Historic Estate
Milford, near Stafford ST17 0XB
www.shugborough.org.uk

Sudbury Hall – The National Trust Museum of Childhood
Sudbury Hall, Ashbourne, Derbyshire DE6 5HT
www.nationaltrust.org.uk

The Tenement House
145 Buccleuch Street, Garnethill, Glasgow G3 6QN
www.nts.org.uk

Town House Museum
46 Queens Street, Kings Lynn PE30 1HX
www.museums.norfolk.gov.uk

York Castle Museum
Eye of York, York YO1 9RY
www.yorkcastlemuseum.org.uk

INDEX

These are the lists of contents for each title in *A Victorian Childhood:*

At Home
The move to towns • Homes for poor people • Suburbs • Comfortable homes • Heat and light • Washing and baths • Families • Babies • Health and illness • Clothes • Keeping in touch

At Play
The nursery • Indoor play • Pastimes • Sundays • Outdoor fun • Sports • Street games • Entertainment • Outings • Holidays • The Seaside

At School
Early schools • Schools for all • The classroom • The school day • Learning to write • Other subjects • Boys' lessons • Girls' lessons • Exercise and hygiene • Absences • Punishments and rewards

At Work
Child workers • Nasty jobs • On the farm • In the home • Cottage industries • Shop boys • Street sellers • Guttersnipes • Scavengers • Helping children • Schools